by kyle & groot

Cooper's Pack Publishing

Cooper's Pack, New York City is a work of fiction. Any resemblance to real people or animals, stuffed or otherwise, is purely coincidental.

All the animals had fun in the writing of this book.

Copyright © 2007
by kyle & groot / A.R.T

All rights reserved.

ISBN-13: 978-0-9794882-0-7
ISBN-10: 0-9794882-0-6

Library of Congress
Control Number: 2007906164

All rights reserved, including the right to reproduce the book or portions thereof in any form whatsoever. No part of Cooper's Pack may be stored, reproduced, or transmitted by any means, electronic, mechanical, photocopying, recording, or otherwise without written permission from the authors.

For user permissions, special discounts for bulk purchases, custom activity books, and/or ancillary information, visit CoopersPack.com or contact Cooper's Pack Publishing at Cooper@CoopersPack.com or 877-278-3278.

Cooper's Pack is a registered trademark of kyle & groot, along with A.R.T.

The Secretary of State
of the United States of America
hereby requests all whom it may concern to permit the citizen/
national of the United States named herein to pass
without delay or hindrance and in case of need to
give all lawful aid and protection.

Le Secrétaire d'Etat
des Etats-Unis d'Amérique
prie par les présentes toutes autorités compétentes de laisser passer
le citoyen ou ressortissant des Etats-Unis titulaire du présent passeport,
sans délai ni difficulté et, en cas de besoin, de lui accorder
toute aide et protection légitimes.

COOPER

SIGNATURE OF BEARER/SIGNATURE DU TITULAIRE/FIRMA DEL TITULAR

NOT VALID UNTIL SIGNED

PASSPORT

USA

UNITED STATES OF AMERICA

Type / Type / Tipo: P
Code / Code / Código: USA
Passport No. / No. du Passeport / No. de Pasaporte: 0150619420

Surname / Nom / Apellidos

Given names / Prénoms / Nombres

Nationality / Nationalité / Nacionalidad
UNITED STATES OF AMERICA

Date of birth / Date de naissance / Fecha de nacimiento
Jun 19

Sex / Sexe / Sexo: M
Place of birth / Lieu de naissance / Lugar de nacimiento

Date of issue / Date de délivrance / Fecha de expedición
05 Feb 2006

Date of expiration / Date d' expiration / Fecha de caducidad
04 Feb 2016

Authority / Autorité / Autoridad
Seattle

Amendments / Modifications / Enmiendas
See Page 24

P<USACO<<OPER<<<<<<<<<<<<<<<<<<<<<<<<<<<<<<<<<<<<<<<<<<<<<<<

24

001515387USA151506190<<<<<<<<<<<<387<<<<<<<<<<<<<<<<<<<06

Phinney called the other day
and invited me to visit him
in New York City.
I haven't seen that crazy
bear in years!
ARGENTINA
NEW YORK
The Great Northwest
LONDON, ENGLAND
Canada
Traveling the Alps
Castles in Europe
Amsterdam

Phinney

I first met Phinney at camp where we burned marshmallows and sailed around the lake.

Phinney is a great goalie!

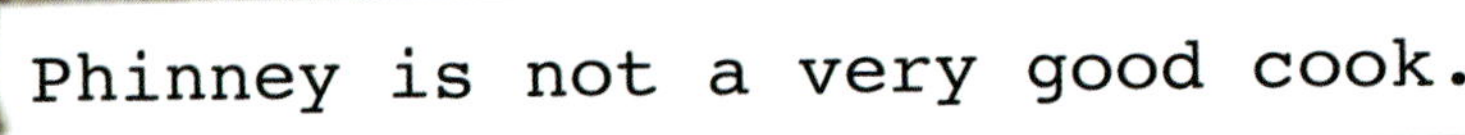

Phinney is not a very good cook.

At night Phinney would tell me about travels with his family to far away places.

His stories were amazing and always made me want to learn more.

I even started dreaming about where I would like to visit...

Can I climb all the way up the Eiffel Tower?
Does spaghetti taste better in Italy?
Can I sit on top of the great pyramids of Egypt?
Can I rollerblade on the Great Wall of China?
Do they have my favorite sugar cookies in Timbuktu?

When I was growing up, my grandfather used to tell me about his adventures around the world.
He has been everywhere.
I haven't been anywhere…
but I can change that!
WELCOME TO
GIBRALTAR
IMMIGRATION DEPT
PERMIT
DAYS
COPENHAGEN
KØBENHAVN
022
上陸許可
入国審査官・日本国
JAPAN
在留資格
短期滞在
Status : Temporary Visitor
在留期間
Duration : 90 days
NARITA(1)
JAPANIMMIGRATION
THE PASSPORT BEARER TO
PASSKONTROLLEN
ARLANDA
2001-01-14
INREST SVERIGE
ICELAND
RIGA
Nº
Canada
CUSTOMS DOUANES
901
CANADA
NIAGARA FALLS
427
The Friendly Island
ST. MAARTEN
IMMIGRATION
No.4
In
Out
IRELA
DUBLIN AIRP

STAY IN PORT
IMMIGRATION (MALTA) - 29
MALTA
AIR TERMINAL
ARRIVAL - 29
NL
AMSTERDAM
Praha
PRAGUE
JAMAICA
LANDED
JAMAICA
ROME
MALPENSA
DEPARTMENT OF IMMIGRATION
WELCOME TO THE
CAYMAN ISLANDS
D
DUSSELDORF
IMMIGRATION OFFICER
SCOTLAND
GLASGOW
SCHWEIZ
SWITERLAND
ZURICH-FLUGHAFEN
ANGUILLA WEST INDIES
ENTRY BY SEA
ANGUILLA
Employment Prohibited
24
I thought it over and decided to visit Phinney.
In fact I might just keep going!
I will have to get a ticket.
What else do I need?
Where else should I go?
Maybe my grandfather could help me...

I called Grandpa the next day.

He said he was going to send me the most important thing any world traveler needs.

What was it?

I had no idea but he said it would be perfect.

He also suggested I get a passport so I could visit all of the places on my list after New York.

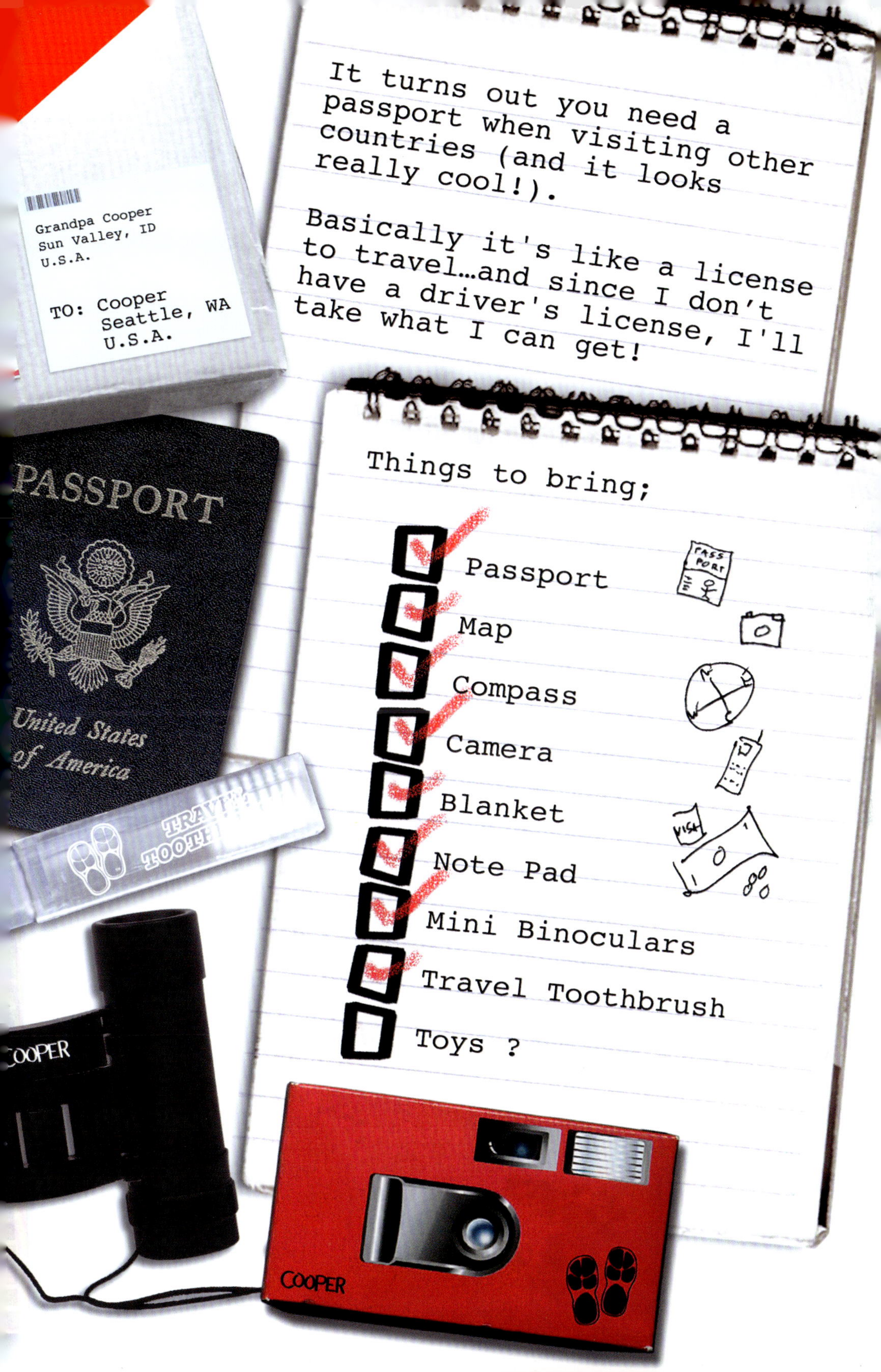
Grandpa Cooper
Sun Valley, ID
U.S.A.
TO: Cooper
Seattle, WA
U.S.A.
It turns out you need a passport when visiting other countries (and it looks really cool!).
Basically it's like a license to travel…and since I don't have a driver's license, I'll take what I can get!
Things to bring;
Passport
Map
Compass
Camera
Blanket
Note Pad
Mini Binoculars
Travel Toothbrush
Toys ?
PASSPORT
United States of America
TRAVEL TOOTH
COOPER
COOPER

A package arrived the next day.
My grandfather had sent me a brand new travel pack.
I immediately called Phinney to tell him I was on my way to NYC (the Big Apple).
little apple
Pacific Standard Time
ABC
Phinney
917.555.56
Options
Eastern Standard Time
Cooper
1.206.555.7225

dpa Coo
Valley
.A.
O: Cooper
Seattle,
U.S
It was 1:39 in the afternoon when I called Phinney, which means it was 4:39 PM his time, because of the time zone difference. There are 24 standard time zones in the world, each spaced by an hour.
Phinney said he was excited to see me tomorrow.
I finished packing (thank you Grandpa!).
Here we go...

With my ticket in paw, I got on the plane and fastened my seatbelt (which was almost as large as me!).
AIRways
E-TICKET
COOPER
SEATTLE TA
NEW YORK C
AW 6
G
MAR
N10
830A
037 75362111
Departing Flight Information
AIRways
Flight 6
5h 27m, 2841 mi
Seattle Tacoma Intl (SEA)
Seattle, WA
Departs: 9:00 AM
To
day, March 16, 2
Departing Flight Information
AIRways
Flight 1
6h 19m, 312
To
The plane.

Aircraft
Boeing 767 (Jet)
Economy/Coach

Aircraft
Boeing 767 (Jet)
Economy/Coach

New York City.

I am almost there.

Statue of Liberty.

I definitely recommend the window seat.

After five hours of flying, I could see the New York skyline.

Phinney texted me to meet him at Grand Central, a famous train station in New York City.

So I took a taxi cab and headed into the city.

There were cabs everywhere!

Fun Facts

There are 12,000 taxi cabs in New York City.

To catch a cab, look for numbers on the roof.

If they are lit up, the cab is available.

Hold your arm up and hope they see you…

I arrived at Grand Central where I saw Phinney smiling and waving (it's hard to miss a bear waving on the street!).

After my long flight it was great to see a familiar face.

My taxi.

Fun Facts
Title on building reads: Grand Central Terminal.
Over 150,000 people travel through Grand Central each day. That is a lot of people!
Opened in 1913.
EXPRESS MAIL

The buildings make me feel really small.
Phinney decided to give me a tour of the city.
We walked over to the Empire State Building, one of the most famous landmarks in New York City (and the world).

Fun Facts
Empire State Building
Built in 1930-31
102 Floors
1,453 Feet Tall
(443 Meters)
Wow! What a view!
After the longest elevator ride of my life, Phinney and I stopped to take in the sights from the 86th floor observation deck.
The people on the street looked like ants.

After visiting the Empire State Building, we wandered around to see what else we could find.

We found ourselves walking through Times Square, surrounded by the largest TV screens I had ever seen.
They were bigger than my house.
Phinney called this area a tourist trap but it looked cool to me (I even bought a souvenir).
BRANDON
TAKE HOME A MEMORY
Share Moments. Share Life.

Fun Facts

Times Square is actually shaped like a bow tie (not a square)!

Over 11 million people visit Times Square each year.

Phinney and I walk through Times Square.

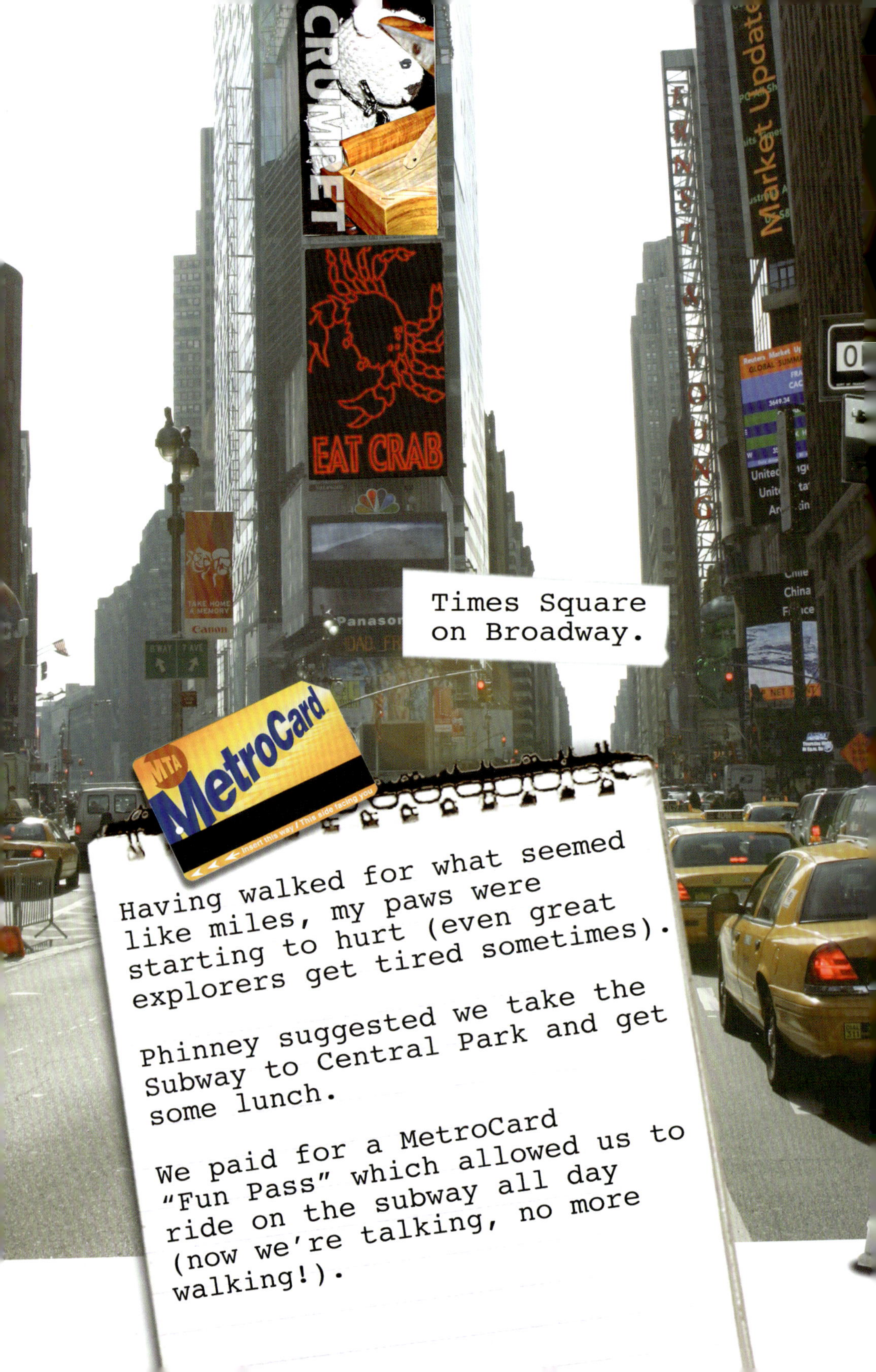

Times Square on Broadway.

Having walked for what seemed like miles, my paws were starting to hurt (even great explorers get tired sometimes).

Phinney suggested we take the Subway to Central Park and get some lunch.

We paid for a MetroCard "Fun Pass" which allowed us to ride on the subway all day (now we're talking, no more walking!).

While we were entering the subway, Phinney pointed out that he knew the person in the ad... "That's my buddy L.L.", he said.

Phinney must know some cool people.

The N train to Central Park.

We got off the subway near Central Park and found a hotdog stand.

They seem to be everywhere in New York City.

There are also people selling pretzels, t-shirts, and even watches on the street.

Hotdog stand.

Fun Facts

There are over 3,000 Hot Dog Stands in NYC.

Central Park is the largest park in NYC.

Phinney and I enjoyed our lunch.

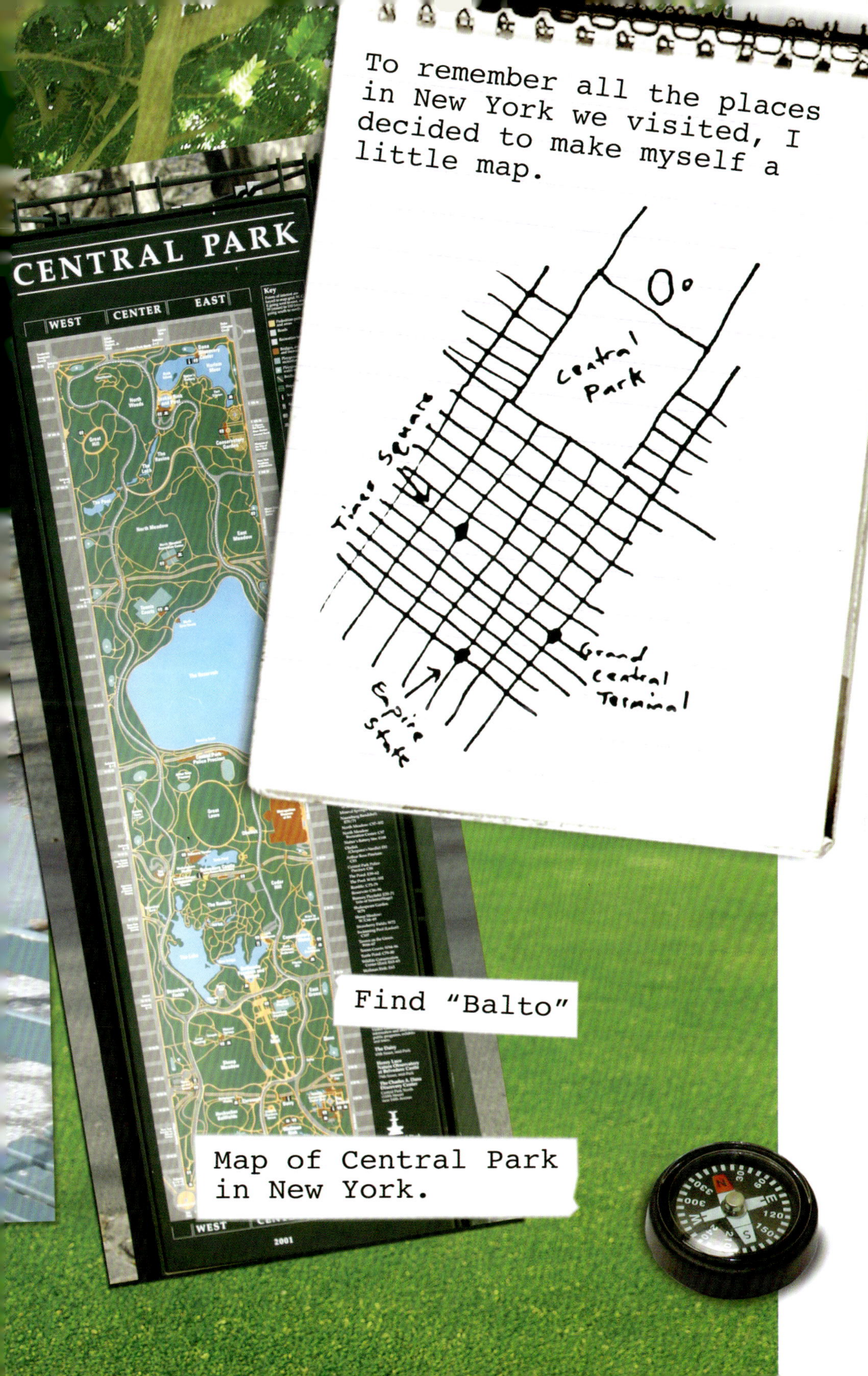
To remember all the places in New York we visited, I decided to make myself a little map.
0°
Central Park
Times Square
Grand Central Terminal
Empire State
CENTRAL PARK
WEST
CENTER
EAST
Find "Balto"
Map of Central Park in New York.
WEST
2001
N
E
S
W
30
60
120
150
210
240
300
330

One of many bridges
in Central Park.
Fun Facts - Central Park
Contains two ice rinks, a
zoo, 21 playgrounds, 26
ballfields, and a carousel.
58 miles of walking paths
with 36 bridges and arches.

After lunch we walked through the park. It is amazing how many things you can do in New York City.

We took a rest and posed for a picture. A nice tourist offered to take one of us if we would take one of him and his family (...of course!).

We sat in a tree for awhile (because that is what city bears do) and talked about my journey.

I told Phinney how I wanted to use my passport and see the rest of the world, including London, Paris, Bangkok, Rome, and Tokyo.

Phinney suggested a few things to remember when traveling:
·Have fun and take pictures.
·Be courteous and respectful to others.
·Be smart and learn about new cultures.
·Make new friends.

London, UK
Flight 22
We went back to Phinney's apartment and he showed me his recent travel photos, including some from London, England.

Phinney thought I should visit London for my next stop.

He said the city was great and since they speak English it would help me for my first international trip.

I used Phinney's computer and bought a ticket to London for the next morning.

I couldn't believe I was off to England!

I thanked Phinney for
showing me New York.
What a great day we had...
tall buildings, subways,
and people everywhere.
It was a top dog day!

My dreams were filled with world travels and adventure.

The next morning Phinney took me to the airport and said he had a surprise for me.
He had e-mailed his buddy L.L. and arranged for him to meet me in London.
How cool is that!?!
Ticketing/Check-In

Stockholm
Gothenburg
Helsinki
London
Stuttgart
Phinney points to where I am going.
airLINES
Phinney wished me well and reminded me to look for the only lamb wearing a tie at the airport in London...
That would be L.L.

It was so great to see Phinney.

I wished he could have come with me.

Instead, he said he would meet me somewhere on my journey.

I can't wait!

I am on my way to London.

New York City
(North America)

"The Pond"

Some people call the
Atlantic Ocean "The Pond".
(Ireland)
(UK)
London
(Europe)

WE GO EVERYWHERE

I put my souvenir postcard in my pack and decided to start a collection.
Then I thought about my journey ahead.
More importantly...
What were they serving for lunch?
London here I come!

ATLAS

COOPER'S PACK™
ACTIVITIES
BUM

Seattle, Washington
This is my local beach.
My living room.
My favorite sport is soccer.
Seattle
El. 125 ft.
Chico
303

COOPER'S PACK™
NEW YORK CITY
The Space Needle.
I love boating too!
More to Explore:
Create a scrapbook showing your hometown and favorite things to do!
After your travels, see if your favorite activities have changed.

Amsterdam, Netherlands
Seattle, WA.
My home town.
London, England
Paris, France
New York City, NY.
Where Phinney lives.
Timbuktu, Mali
Rio de Janeiro, Brazil
Santiago, Chile
Cape Town,
South Africa
More to Explore:
Draw a map of the world.
Locate and write in the names of all the cities you have visited or places you would like to go.

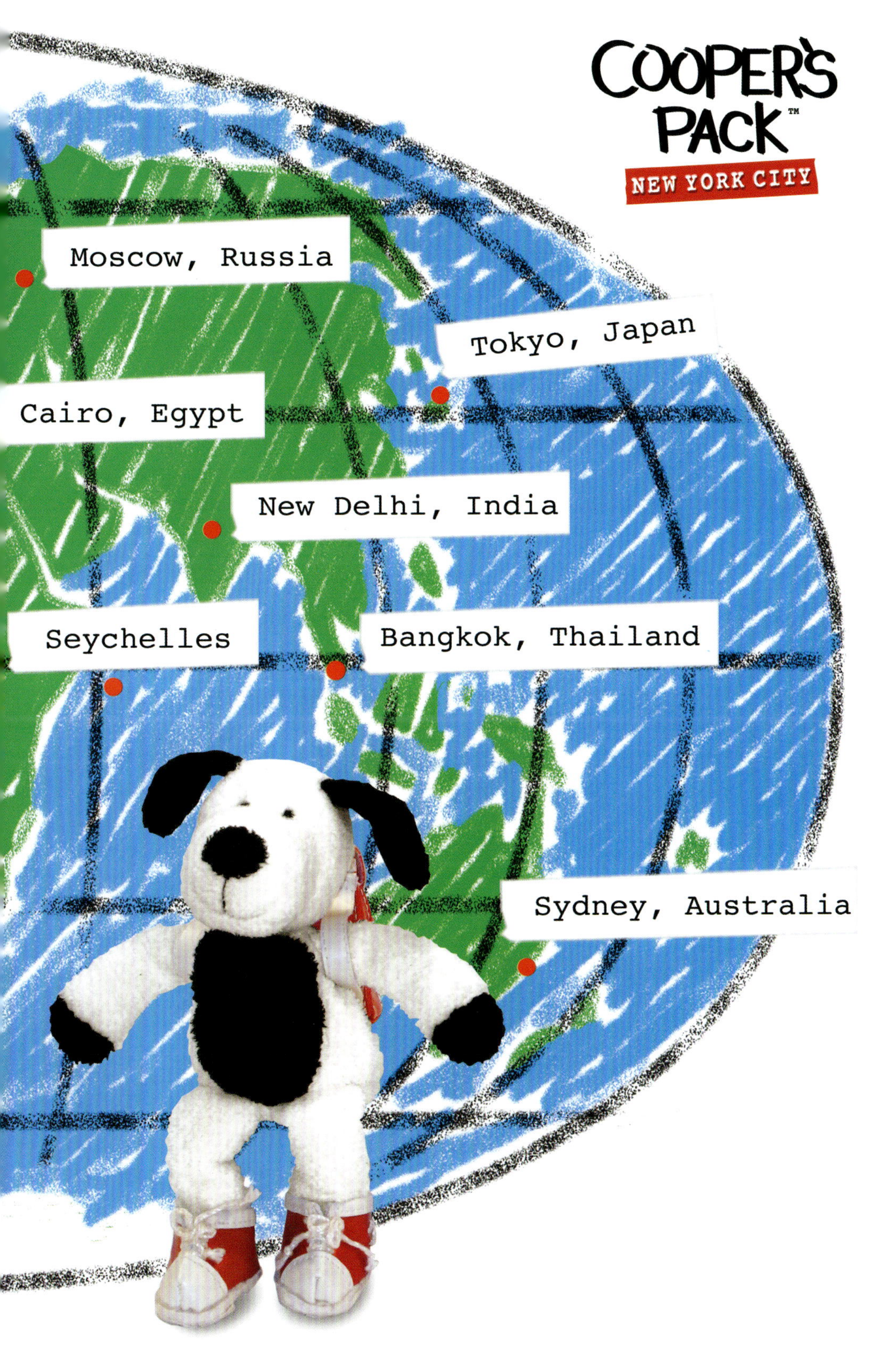
COOPER'S PACK™
NEW YORK CITY
Moscow, Russia
Tokyo, Japan
Cairo, Egypt
New Delhi, India
Seychelles
Bangkok, Thailand
Sydney, Australia

+10
Anchorage
Edmonton
+7
+6
+8
Winnipeg
Seattle, WA. 12:00 noon.
Seattle
Denver
Chicago
Wash.
COOPER'S PACK™
NEW YORK CITY
San Francisco
Los Angeles
Hous.
New Orleans
Tropic of Cancer
+10
Honolulu
Mexico City
Equator.
Fun Facts:
There are 24 standard time zones in the world, just like the 24 hours in a day.
Russia has 11 time zones.
China has only one time zone.

London, England. 8:00 PM
New York City, NY. 3:00 PM
More to Explore:
Locate a time zone map or website.
When it is 7:00 PM where you live, what time will it be in:
A friend or relative's town?
Paris, France?
Phinney's apartment in NYC?

More to Explore:

Get a copy of an up-to-date map for the subway.

QUEENS
BROOKLYN
FLUSHING
KEW GARDENS HILLS
HILLCREST
REGO PARK
FOREST HILLS
KEW GARDENS
RICHMOND HILL
GLENDALE
OCEAN HILL-BROWNSVILLE
EAST NEW YORK
CROWN HEIGHTS
EAST FLATBUSH
FLATBUSH
FLATLANDS
MIDWOOD
SHEEPSHEAD BAY
BRIGHTON BEACH
CONEY ISLAND
BREEZY POINT
ROCKAWAY PARK
Jamaica Bay
63 Dr Rego Park
67 Av
Forest Hills 71 Av
75 Av
Kew Gardens Union Tpke
Briarwood/ Van Wyck Blvd
Middle Village Metropolitan Av
Fresh Pond Rd
Forest Av
Seneca Av
Woodhaven Blvd
85 St-Forest Pkwy
75 St
Cypress Hills
Crescent St
Norwood Av
Cleveland St
Van Siclen Av
Alabama Av
104 St
111 St
Halsey St
Wilson Av
Bushwick Av Aberdeen St
Chauncey St
Gates Av
Broadway Junction
Atlantic Av
Liberty Av
Van Siclen Av
Rockaway Av
Ralph Av
Utica Av
Sutter Av
Junius St
Livonia Av
Saratoga Av
Sutter Av-Rutland Rd
Crown Hts Utica Av
Kingston Av
Sterling St
Winthrop St
Church Av
Beverly Rd
Newkirk Av
Brooklyn College Flatbush Av
Cortelyou Rd
Avenue H
Avenue J
Avenue M
Kings Hwy
Avenue U
Neck Rd
Sheepshead Bay
Brighton Beach
Ocean Pkwy
West 8 St NY Aquarium
Coney Island Stillwell Av
Avenue N
Avenue P
Avenue X
Neptune Av
Gravesend 86 St
25 Av
Bay 50 St
Beach 90 St
Beach 98 St
Beach 105 St
Rockaway Park Beach 116 St
New York City Transit
Manhattan Subway Map
February 2004
COOPER'S PACK
NEW YORK CITY

COOPERSPACK.COM
More to Explore:
Keep a journal of where you went on your trip.
Use the journal to map the places you visited and the things you saw.
Places I visited:
Grand Central Terminal
Empire State Building
Times Square
Central Park
Other places to see...
Theatres on Broadway
Madison Square Garden
Brooklyn Bridge
Rockefeller Center
Chinatown
Little Italy
Wall Street
United Nations
Chrysler Building
Metropolitan Museum
South Street Seaport
Guggenheim Museum
Columbia University

Central Park.
Times Square.
Grand Central Terminal.
Empire State Building.
COOPER'S PACK™
NEW YORK CITY

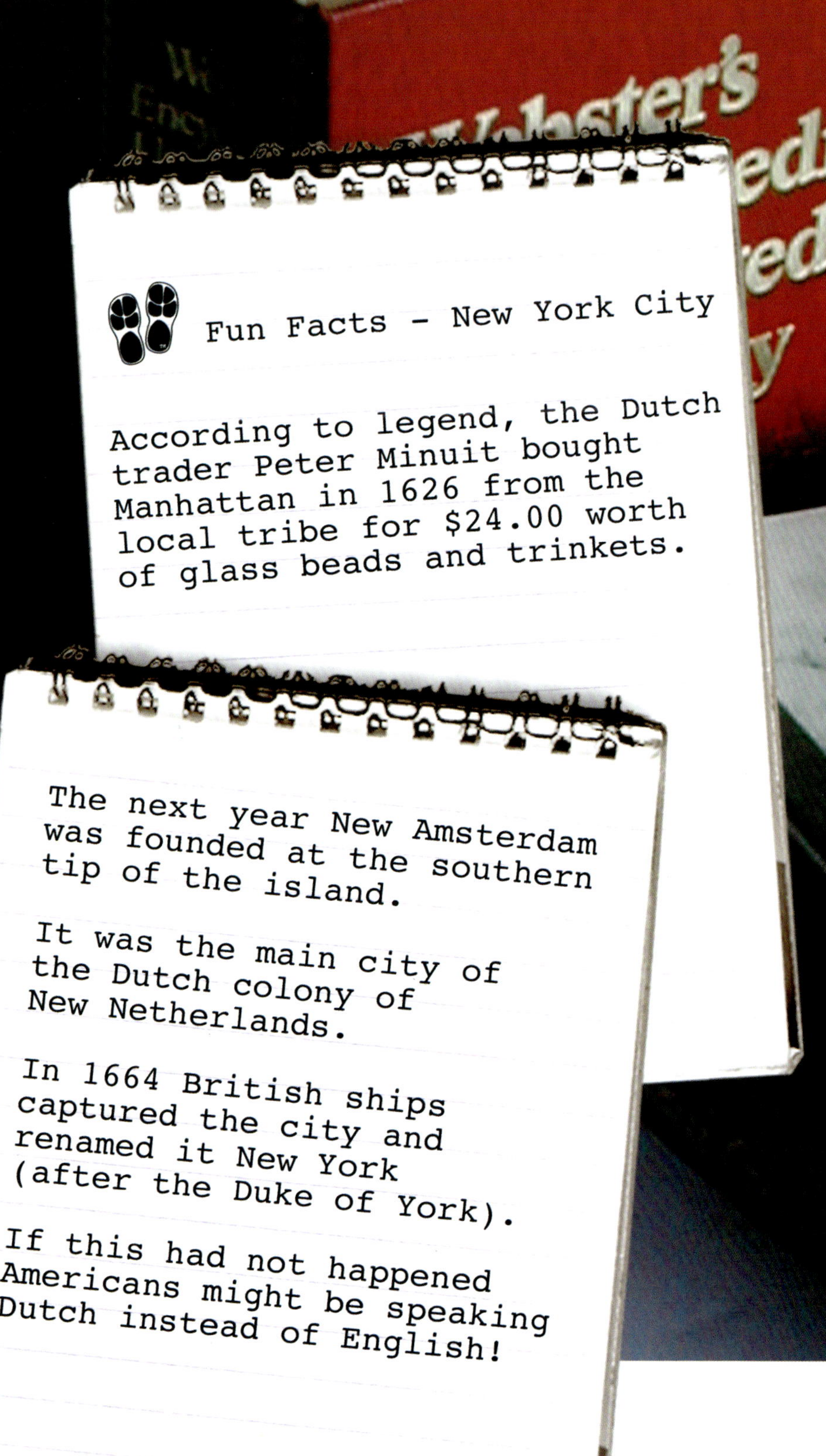
Fun Facts - New York City
According to legend, the Dutch trader Peter Minuit bought Manhattan in 1626 from the local tribe for $24.00 worth of glass beads and trinkets.
The next year New Amsterdam was founded at the southern tip of the island.
It was the main city of the Dutch colony of New Netherlands.
In 1664 British ships captured the city and renamed it New York (after the Duke of York).
If this had not happened Americans might be speaking Dutch instead of English!

COOPER'S PACK
ADVENTURES
Over 8,000,000 people live in New York City making it the largest city in the U.S. and twelfth in the world.
The city is made up of five boroughs, including Manhattan, The Bronx, Queens, Brooklyn, and Staten Island.
COOPER'S PACK™
NEW YORK CITY

Some currency used in the United States of America:

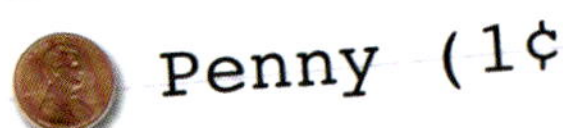

Penny (1¢)

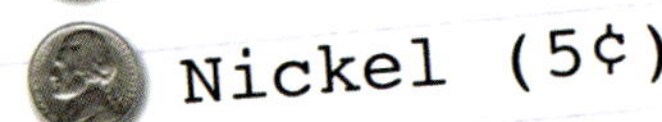

Nickel (5¢)

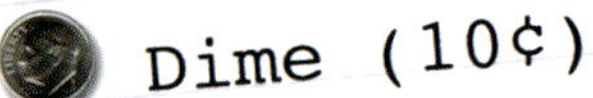

Dime (10¢)

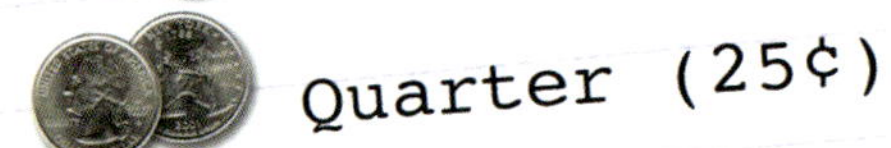

Quarter (25¢)

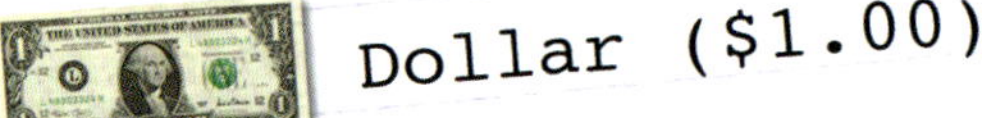

Dollar ($1.00)

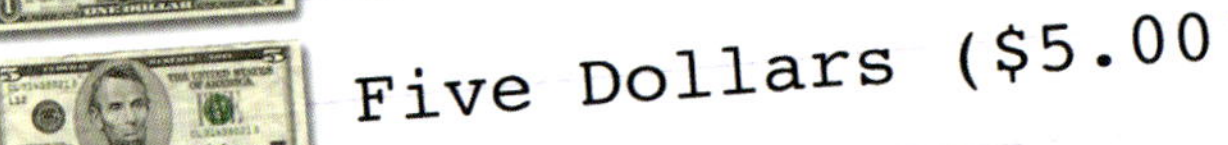

Five Dollars ($5.00)

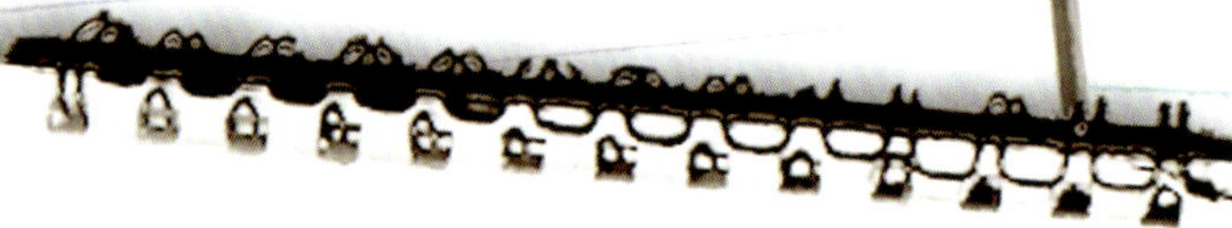

Local Information:

Lexington Avenue is refered to as "Lex".

I ❤ NY is "I Love New York"

Get an All-Day MetroCard for the subway.

Manhattan Island is 13 miles long (22 km).

In Manhattan, "uptown" means north and "downtown" means south.

ruary 12

think I was the
ortest person on the
ubway today. Oh well.
The people were nice.

Phinney is funny but
I think he needs to
take a bath more often.
I need to remember to
send him some soap.
Oh, and a thank you
note!

COOPER'S PACK™
NEW YORK CITY

More to Explore:

Get a journal and write down notes about the city you are going to visit.

Keep making notes as you travel around the city (and the world!).

More to Explore:

Start a scrap book or build a website to share your pictures with family and friends.

COOPER'S PACK™
NEW YORK CITY

Phinney and I inside Grand Central Terminal.

A top dog building near Times Square.

More to Explore:

Take a variety of pictures showing the city and where you visited.

Don't forget the art!

Buying our hotdogs.

The New York Public Library.

The building Phinney lives in.

COOPER'S PACK™

NEW YORK CITY

Name: Cooper
Height: 6"
Weight: 8oz
Eye Color: Black
Born: Olympic Mountains (outside of Seattle, WA)

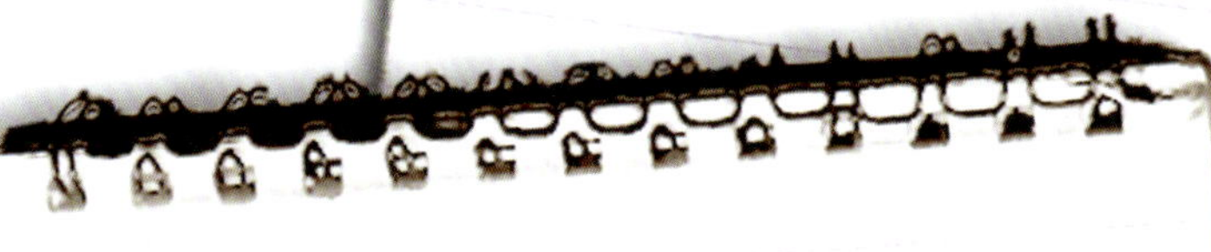

Favorites:

Foods: T-bone steak, milk
Color: Navy blue
Places: Hiking, Pacific Ocean, Grandpa's house
Books: A Separate Peace
Artist: Marcus Bausch, Jr.
Teacher: Mr. Axling(Geography)
Class: Geography
Music: Phish, Pete Droge
Sports: Soccer, skiing, hackysack, boating
Hobbies: Map collecting
Sayings: "Top Dog"
Nicknames: Coop

Name: Phinneus (Phinney)
Height: 8"
Weight: 1 lb
Eye Color: Black
Born: Near a pumpkin patch in upstate New York

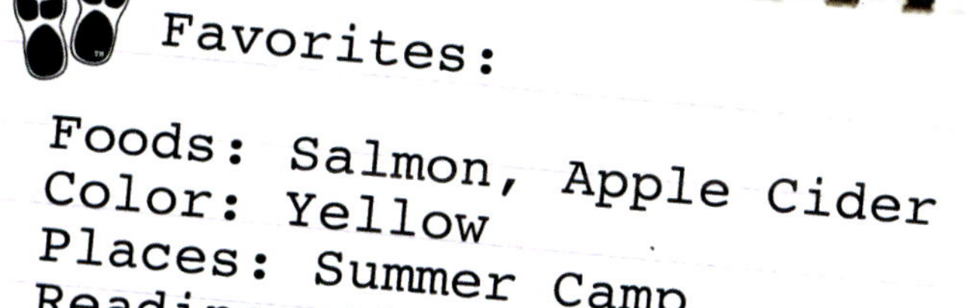

Favorites:

Foods: Salmon, Apple Cider
Color: Yellow
Places: Summer Camp
Reading: The New York Times
Artist: Brian Rudd
Teacher: Mrs. Feroy (Art)
Class: Sculpture
Music: Beautiful South, Housemartins
Sports: Swimming, golf, Cooper's games
Hobbies: Creating art & sculptures
Saying: "Where's my kitty… the little kitty?"
Nickname: That Bear!

Insert your photo here.
Name:
Height:
Weight:
Eye Color:
Born:
Languages:
Favorites:
Places:
Books:
Music:
Sayings:
Nickname:

Travel Information:

Date: ______________________

Destination(s): ______________________

____

____

Transportation: ______________________

____

 More to Explore:

Create a record of your travels, including what you are like and where you are traveling.

This will be fun to read many years from now :)

Send Cooper your travel stories, highlights and photos of your stuffed animal friend(s) to:

Cooper@CoopersPack.com

You may find them featured on Cooper's website, including updates and additional pictures of Cooper's adventures.

Credits:

Central Park Map
H Plus Incorporated
Pleasantville, NY

MTA New York City Subway Map
Metropolitan Transportation Authority

Original artwork in Cooper's and Phinney's apartments by Brian Rudd

kyle

Making things happen.

groot

Living XXlarge on the Beach.